The Art of Departure

Chris, 2/18

The Art of Departure

Poems by

Maureen Sherbondy

*Best wishes
Thanks for listening.*

Maureen Sh—

Kelsay Books

© 2015 Maureen Sherbondy. All rights reserved. This material may not be reproduced in any form, published, reprinted, recorded, performed, broadcast, rewritten or redistributed without the explicit permission of Maureen Sherbondy. All such actions are strictly prohibited by law.

Cover Art (istockphoto.com)

ISBN 13:978-0692533482

Kelsay Books
Aldrich Press
www.kelsaybooks.com

Acknowledgments

Big Table Publishing: "Cupid Returns to Recover His Arrow"
Broad River Review: "Pining for Old Lovers"
Carolina Woman: "Jill Gains Her Independence," "The Vanishing"
Connotation Press: "Meditation on Leaving"
Dry Creek Review: "Wedding Gifts as Warning Signs"
Fjords: "All Because of Her Husband's Hearing Loss"
Iodine: "This Place We Are in Our Marriage"
RiverSedge: "Mr. Potato Head"
Spring Garden Press: "Grief Basket," "Limbo," "Unresolved"
Walter Magazine: "This Is Your Life"
When Women Waken: "Arrow," "The Still Tongue," "I Will Not," "Replaced"

Contents

Acknowledgments

Meditation on Leaving

Meditation on Leaving	13
The Art of Departure	15
This Place We Are at in Our Marriage	16
Mr. Potato Head	17
Enough	18
Five and One	19
Arrow	20
Reason	21
Wedding Gifts as Warning Signs	22
Dick and Jane	23
Departure and Return	24
Cupid Returns to Recover His Arrow	25
The Still Tongue	26
Demanding Honesty from a Liar	27
Turned Sour	28
This Is a Test	29
Answers	30
All Because of Her Husband's Hearing Loss	31
Limbo	32
Unresolved	33
I Will Not	34
Green Basil Leaves	35
Division of Assets	36
Replaced	37
The Torching of Loveland	38
Scarecrow	39
Loveland Finale	40

This Is Your Life Now

Jill Gains Her Independence	43
Ocean Wrestle	44
Geese Resting on the Median	45
Every Act Leads to This	46
Home Show	47
What to Assume of the Single Man at Mid-Life	49
The Vanishing	50
Fly	51
On the Road to Wendell, a Rainbow	52
Memory's Innkeeper	53
This Is Your Life	54
Spell of Larimar	55
Stinger	56
Grief Basket	57
Dream Rant	60
Train, Remains	63
At the Midnight Carnival	64
Drill, Baby	65
Museum of Lost Wishes	67
This After Place	68
Accounting (9 Dates in 9 Days)	69
Make No Exceptions	71
Pining for Old Lovers	72
Collage: Legs and Arms	73

About the Author

Meditation on Leaving

Meditation on Leaving

I don't want to mention death
anymore or the black bird swooping down
from the pine tree. I need daffodils
to poke their sharp heads through winter's ground,
for the purple clematis to vine-climb around
the mailbox post and Carolina wrens to visit my deck.
It is not time says the moon. So I place my hand
on your cold grave, set a stone down again
and wait for spring to whisper in.

I find a brown leaf in the grass, a gray bird
twisted on the ground,
flat snakes, dead branches.
I close my eyes and dreams will not return.
Just my father's voice replaying in my head
repeating the same sentence again and again.

On my wedding day he stood beside me,
hands dead at his side; he forgot to lift
my white veil to reveal my unmarried self. I lifted
the lace myself. Now my hands are so weighed
down, I do not know how to lift this black veil
that has sewed itself into my face.

What was there before departure?
I watch fathers greet daughters,
grandparents sweeping up grandchildren.
Lips meeting cheeks.

I have been here a long time at this gate waiting for arrival
that will never come again. Now leaving is all there is.

The mother coming through the front screen door in summer,
groceries in hand, flies buzzing through. A lover beside her.
Those three brothers back from college or work or a friend's.
Even the dog returned after a daylong escape. How does it shift?
The door slamming on the way out, the father packing,
the suitcase in his hand, the not coming back.

The tumblers will not click into place, numbers flit by in the sky,
I can no longer reach them. My arms are not long enough.
Must I grow wings to fling this feathered body to meet
the ones and the sixes. How can a number matter?
21 years of marriage, 3 children, 1 dog. 5 houses.
It could have been anyone on any given day. Why pick
that man on that train? Why take away this father?

I am walking backwards trying to reverse the hands
of the clock. Nothing works. I stand in a tree and sweep
the sky with a net; numbers fall inside. Let's turn that lock again.

The month my father died the black bird returned
to my windowsill. It was all about the leaving. The brothers left
the house long before. The mother, the father. Now it's my turn.
I want to go. I don't want to go. A different house.
A different form of death. I am grabbing
the knob, pushing through the door.

And all those stones I set on my father's grave
have somehow turned up inside my own pocket.

The Art of Departure

There is an art to departure:
wear a grin on your face,
chin up, shoulders back.
Walk slowly. Memorize
the house, the walls, the faces.
Turn the knob, meander out
as if you'll be back later,
as if you're just wandering
up the driveway to gather
another day's delivered mail.

This Place We Are at in Our Marriage

This place we are at in our marriage
is like Newark – you have to land there
but it smells bad. Something is rotting;
it's gray and smoky; you want to leave
as soon as you arrive.

This is a transition place between
lovely suburban New Jersey towns
and the exciting big city. You can see
the tall buildings in the distance,
but it's hard to enjoy anything while
the toxic fumes assault your senses.

No one told you about it, that to get
to Broadway, to entertainment, theatre,
and gourmet food, you'd spend years in Newark
limbo, lost, trying to figure out how
to exit and arrive where you want to end up.

Mr. Potato Head

Mr. Potato Head sits on my desk
mocking me again. Old wedding
photos collect dust on the shelf.
All is broken. Shut off. Loveless
louse of winter. Ball bug. I curl up,
hide inside this shuttered house.

Once I would rearrange this face
for you. Ear to eye, nose to mouth.
What difference really in this final
season. Iced-over eyes and reason.
Soon, it will not matter. The ground
is too hard to bury the dead.

Mr. Potato Head in the closet now;
no roots sprout from his plastic
body. Searching for a way out,
I have been too long in this dark
closet beside him. Doorknob gone,
hands removed from our sides,
no way to even open the door.

Enough

It would have been enough,
the lemon scent of your skin
your long fingers stroking the nape of my neck,
the river of my hair streaming down
your chest. My hands in your hair
dark as southern tree bark at midnight.

Night after night this slice, this baptism,
this dipping of body into body, the moan
in the droning silence. Behind the bedroom
window the sound of a dog barking
for his misplaced bone or lost home, and a necklace
of faraway stars waiting for someone to look up.
A river flows beneath the stars.

You and I are now lost in a waterway flailing,
our arms apart, disparate and desperate.
Once we floated in the same boat, moving
forward toward an island we could almost see.
Once we were enough. Not now.

Those small stones from the river
rolled and folded one into the other.
The fluid movement of our hips,
our bodies, once pushing the water away
now drowns us. Now the stones have formed
a boulder between us. How can we
reach up and climb onto what keeps us apart.
I am grinding away at the boulder trying to break
the giant into smaller parts, to set it back in the river
silt. But it is too late and we together are not enough.

Five and One

Five geese stride and bob across the grass,
always this group of five seen on my morning
outing. I wander alone everywhere now.

Years ago in Paris when I spoke no French
I learned to order five of everything
cinq my finger pointed at warm croissants and baguettes
in the patisserie, rolled off my tongue like a true Parisian.
It was enough to know that single word.

Now I'm done with five. The geese march on
in front of me. One stands outside the group;
one by one we wait here. Both of us have left
our troop of five to become a solitary one, an *une*.

Arrow

All you want to do is fly away
from the trees you planted years before,
from the house collecting boxes
in the attic's dust, to flit away from fleeting
time. The husband snores in a shared bed
but you no longer know him. Overnight
some old man robbed his body and mind,
left behind an imposter in the four-post
bed. What was it you once desired?
A brick house on a quiet tree-lined street?
Sweet babies asleep in their beds?
In front of you a door you have a key to,
ridged metal leaves an achy red imprint in your palm.
Now you must knock from the outside
because you are just a stranger.
You want to bury the key in the yard,
to shoot an arrow into the clouds,
watch it land near a different town,
a different house, a different man.

Reason

I repeat the reason until my tongue
grows numb. You do not understand
or even hear my words. It's as if birds
landed, one in each waiting ear
blocking off all sense and sound.

I could stand here for years
but it doesn't matter –
the door is still the door,
my hand is on the knob
and I am leaving.

Wedding Gifts as Warning Signs

Those wrapped gifts in disguise
should have been received as warning.
They were offerings, signs, clues
wrapped in silver and gold with deceptive bows.

The money – that there would never be enough,
the crystal vase for flowers – that flowers die,
candlesticks – that wicks eventually burn out,
the matching his and hers towels – that romance
dries out, fine china – that arguments would begin
over who should wash and who should dry,
until the first plate shatters.

When the money has been spent, the plates
thrown across the no-longer-newlywed
rooms, the no-longer-smiling-for-the-camera
crying bride and groom.

No raised print, black and white
formal announcement of termination of union,
just a whisper, lowered eyes and expectations,
tsk, tsk's, moving boxes labeled *his* and *hers*.

Dick and Jane

She's tumbling backwards to Dick and Jane
simplicity when each day turned
in a logical storyline, one page at a time
then another—a subject, a verb.
Dick running, Jane seeing.

Now run-on sentences and unwanted
dialogue fill her diatribe days, paper cuts
her fingers and blood drips everywhere.
See Jane, see Jane's cut, see red, feel
Jane's pain. How has it come to this?

Those first teachers led her to believe
it would always be this way—Jane
and Dick walking and looking, the sun
on their faces, happy thoughts, happy life.

She has been running her whole life
and that shadow will not stop
chasing her. Why didn't her teacher mention
this little fact: Jane is being chased, Jane
is scared. Run, Jane, run! As fast as you can.

Departure and Return

In labor with my first son
my husband left in a huff,
later explaining that the nurse
annoyed him. He just got up without
explanation, left me breathing
in and out, alone, contraction after
contraction, worrying not about the imminent birth
but instead about his coming back.
This is how it went for twenty years –
me ignoring the rush of pain within
the fleshy walls of my own body,
wondering instead about the when and if
of his return at the end of every day.

Cupid Returns to Recover His Arrow

The husband and wife returned home
to discover love had drained out
of their house.

During the night Cupid reappeared
to retrieve his arrow; there was
a shortage; new couplings needed help.

The wife rubbed her back
to soothe the sore opening;
the husband shrugged, then left.

It ended much as it had begun,
suddenly, with some surprise.

The Still Tongue

In this house I no longer live
the man I once loved greets me.

I look at empty walls,
crumb-laced counters,

magnets on the fridge, anywhere
but at his face. Even a nod is not easy.

As if this place we once lived together,
raised our sons, is another country

and I have not yet learned
how to speak the language.

Demanding Honesty from a Liar

I pin your shoulders
against a wall
until you squirm
in my red-hot hands,
until your worm tongue
unravels and spills
its twisted truths.

Turned Sour

Their love pickled in a jar overnight
his and her hearts turned sour,

the bright moon over the house
could not save them, Cupid's arrows

dispersed and splintered inside the dark hours,
stars fell over another lovers' flesh-spooned slumber.

Honeymoon roses once pressed between
her diary pages now crumbled and littered

the marital bed. They woke itchy and rash-
coated unable to remain and recline body

to body. She packed up her bags, burned
the marriage license and left her gold band

sinking to the bottom of the pickle jar
souring with vinegar and floating dead seeds.

This Is a Test

The locks are changed and you
have to stand outside
your happiness.

Draw a circle in the dirt
with your hurt foot; plant
belongings like bulbs.

Here—your wedding photos
and lost passion, old pressed
roses, one Broadway show ticket.

Here—your child's first tooth,
a blue receiving blanket,
his unfinished baby book.

Stand there while it rains
beneath
a black umbrella.

Now wait until someone opens
the door, invites you in –
then walk away again.

Answers

Soon the wife will be gone
and the husband will cry.

Stare at the now, too-large
bed, the wife's empty side.

He'll hug his pillow, sift
through twenty-two years

of places, friends, summer
trips and their children's births.

He will wonder as the full moon
reaches through the dark window

at midnight what he did or didn't do
to make her go. Neither the moon

nor the stars will offer any answers.

All Because of Her Husband's Hearing Loss

The hall light boobs need changing.
There's perspiration and meatboats for stutter.
The duck ter called to give your flood rest results.
Our son will pivot in spoon.
The blog needs to balk.

What humor will come when crime runs away --
when his sense of taste famishes
and his eye height fades the day.

Limbo

Here she is again trying to bend
beneath the limbo bar.
Ghosts hold the pole, one at each end.

In front of her–a midget,
behind her–a stunted child.
Oh, this isn't fair, she mutters.

Life isn't fair, snorts a ghost.
She turns her body into Gumby,
bends into a ball.

Not fair, cries the child.
She eludes the bar and grins.
The midget and the child smack

the wood with their chins and poof –
they're all gone. She rolls away
knowing now she can change her body

into whatever shape it needs to be.

Unresolved

Even in dreams nothing turns out well –
the dog gets cancer, the roof collapses
and I am searching for a new place to call home
alone. Years ago just one dream replayed –
my college PO box waiting, filled
with accumulated letters from lost friends and lovers.
I tried to open the metal door but could not recall the combination.
Sometimes at night old boyfriends would sneak
inside my bed to caress my skin and kiss my lips.
I once looked forward to darkness and its visitors.
Now night life is dark as day life. This house shifting –
the doorframe waving *this way, this way*.

I Will Not

blow away in winter's wind
like the bank papers and ripped
wedding photos. I will not fade
from this town, this cul de sac.
Every day I plan to stand on the lawn
and plant my lion self so when you come
and go my eyes will follow.
I am gathering sticks and acorns
from this scorned yard, building a new house
out of twigs and loss. When the wind dies
down at night, my spewed words
will invade your room, boom
into our bed so loud, the woman
now sleeping beside you will hear
my words, my lion roar.

Green Basil Leaves

wilt in the bag, trapped.
Devoid of air and light, they sag.
Once I thought what grew
on my deck garden could
flavor every dish cooked
in this summer-lit kitchen,
but my tongue is numb, unable
to taste what I set upon it.
The herbs have been plucked
from the dirt and the dirt spilled
onto the drying grass. I am afraid
to peer inside this bag
and retrieve these leaves,
once green, fragrant. Once
so sweet.

Division of Assets

Years they spent accumulating
furniture, bank accounts, babies.
Now it is all about separating,
making two piles labeled his
and hers. Here—the cash,
here—the cars,
here—a chair,
here—a spoon. But what of the living?

Those babies grown into men,
how do you divide loyalty,
love's affiliation?

And that dog who weeps in a corner
searching for the scent of the missing
woman—what to do with him?
A tail for her, raised ears for him.

Recollection of the famous Bible
story where the real mother
gives up her child to save his life.

Here the woman walks out the front door
and gives up every vital thing.

Replaced

A woman stands in my kitchen,
her eyes locked on my eyes.
I am sitting on the deck of the house
I still own, locked out, waiting
for my son on my outdoor
loveseat. I look up at the window and see her.

How many hours did I peer out
that same window? While I washed
breakfast, lunch, dinner dishes
for twenty years, while I held
a warm coffee mug cradled in my hands,
mornings, afternoons, evenings
spent watching the cardinals, the wrens
leaving, the loblolly pines and their shedding.

Now when I look up
a stranger with dark hair, foreigner
from some foreign land filling
my window, she – inside,
me—outside.
This woman in *my* kitchen, drinking coffee
with *my* husband. For a moment
we freeze, then she vanishes
and my husband steps in the doorway
his body blocking her protectively;
his expression says *you are not wanted here.*

And I do not want him anymore but
this house, this woman in my kitchen
bordered in pears and grapes,
and that window, my coffee cup in her hands—
make bile ripen in my throat.

The Torching of Loveland

Is that you kneeling down
with flames on a torch, touching
fire to land you once kissed and tended?
Old friend, old lover, why
are you laughing now, tossing out
your silver band for the fire to devour?

Are you trying to ignite a field lit with hate?
You will burn the poetry of twenty years,
say our life together tumbled into ash
and no stalks of love could grow
on this scorched acre.

You have cast away your wife
and friends, burned
the barn and troughs. No way
to soothe this parched field anymore.
You have wandered off to a distant
farm. The stench of burning
will linger in the air for years.

Scarecrow

A scarecrow now, I stand planted in the scarred field
straw-hollow limbs waiting for crows
that do not land. Fire halted at the stone circle
around my straw legs. Stick in my spineless backside,
I stand day and night tight and strideless, watching
mica ash ruining the seeds. No barn animal sounds
to keep me company anymore, only distant owls and wolves.

I want to run away, but here I am stuck
unable to push this propped parched body
from Loveland. My tucked-in heart lifted away,
today I am just eyes and damage, straw abandonment
unable to view my own future. Why didn't he just burn
me down too? Better up in flames, the blame, the hurt,
than in this straw-empty waiting state.

Loveland Finale

There will be no more laughing here
beneath the moonlight. I will leave behind
a salt river to douse the wild flames.

The animals are dying in the barn.
You closed the gate and locked them in.
I am not allowed to step upon the ashes,
but the cries of the cattle keep me awake.

My bed is miles downstream from where
we started. The river dried up yesterday
and I dream now of those bleating, mooing creatures

drifted down a scorched field, seeds planted
beneath their hoofs now black and dead. Land
that once held promise, animals that gave.
All is slashed and burned beneath the moonlight.

There is sobbing here where laughter once
filled and fed the marriage bed.
I am not allowed to visit here amid red ashes.

You are the one who folded matches inside
your fisted hand, who ignored the sounds of animals
dying in the barn, ignored the crying of your wife
who only wanted new seed planted in this land.

This Is Your Life Now

Jill Gains Her Independence

I tumbled down the hill alone;
really it was a mountain,
there was no Jack beside me,
it was not water at the top
but a wish waiting. I'm not foolish;
everyone knows a bucket set out
in the yard gathers rain. Why climb
a hill for that which comes so easily with patience.
I climbed alone. A star dangled just above
the peak. While reaching for that bright light
I tumbled backwards.
Stardust lingers on my fingers.
My back hurts sometimes but
my wishes have all come true. Jack
can get his own damn star.

Ocean Wrestle

To wash away my fears
of lost children, I sign my sons
up for swim lessons because
once at the ocean
a towering wave pinned
down my thin ten-year-old body.

I recall the drown-swallow of salt
and sand, the crush and punch
of the crashing liquid body,
that long stretch of time

when surface and light
are stolen from reach,
when drowning is so close
I swirled down its dark airless
alley, until a pinhole of grace
spit me out into the enchanted
place of second chances.

Still, an enormous arm lingers
over my shoulders, never
completely releasing
its muscled hold.

Geese Resting on the Median

Geese wait at the median, precarious limbo
island or choice grass land destination.

I cross the street halfway and then
don't know which side to choose.

Aren't we always stuck between
one place and then the next?

On the way to somewhere different,
better. Perhaps this median we wait

at for a light to change or the cars
to clear is where we meant to stand in the end.

Every Act Leads to This

I tried to swallow the wallow of stars
inciting my body to glow from inside out,
but all I did was torch my tongue
soft running sentences burned, then fizzled.

I tried to grasp your heart inside my own
to show the flame of how I felt, but all
that had grown between us swung lost
inside the melting flesh, led to the end
of we, all I had loved and held—now catastrophe.

I then inhaled the petals that lined the yard
so I could derive the walking scent of spring
from every joyous pore, but all I could bring
forward in April and May were barren
stalks, and then, alas, my own decay.

Home Show

Instead of rows of graduation chairs
this time, only aisles of home repair
booths line this convention center—
fix-up the old, or buy it new, granite counter samples,
maple, oak, and cherry cabinets
on display to browse through, appliance
vendors too, the latest heating and cooling
devices, DIRECTV, satellite
and other hedonistic pleasures, jacuzzis,
game room jazz-it-up entertainment
man-cave fillers, rows and rows
stretched before me.

Three consecutive years, for one day
in May, I, *we*, sat thirty rows back,
waiting to say that word *graduate*
with other proud, near gleeful
husbands, wives, grandparents,
families smiling, all looking forward
thrilled at yet another milestone
in this parenting and offspring hurdle.

My boys turned their tassels to the
other side, walked, one by one
blue robed across that stage. I picture
all of it now as I stand caged for this hourly
wage in this crowded lit-up room.
Employed with a plastered smile
in front of bath and shower exhibits,
getting leads, handing out brochures
to prospective customers, homeowners
still, all of them.

One day I woke to find my family dispersed,
gone. My large brick home torn apart, then sold.
Today I spill forth the tumble of the sale, the art
of money earning, wondering all the while,
how and why my own home blew asunder.

What to Assume of the Single Man at Mid-Life

Assume he is married or living with another woman,
that he is seeing someone else and is in love
but just finding what else is out there, what he can get,
that he is gay and acting hetero, that he is angry
at his ex and will take it out on you, that he was dumped
a month earlier and is in no way at all ready
to date, that he has illegitimate children,
that he likes you but will disappear for no reason,
that he has anger problems, a mood disorder, alcohol issues.
He's a sexual predator, an ex-con, owns a gun, is lousy
in the sack, will be a terrible boyfriend, his "consultant" job
really means he hasn't worked in two years. He is actually
scared of strong women. When he says
you aren't right for him, realize that no one will ever be.

The Vanishing

Boyfriends vanish
one by one, fall
along cracks of sidewalks,
inside radio talk programs,
fold their bodies
into ant-sized crumbs
then shimmy feet first down
blades of grass.
They crawl inside metal gutters
beside leaves and twigs,
then jump on top of slanted roof
shingles, flit away into
the gray dusk by skydiving from
planes and helicopters,
they hop onto the wings
of bats and rise up toward
the full moon, they flush
their bodies down toilet
bowls in restaurant bathrooms,
then file down the earth's slopes
and slide off sharp edges
just to get away from what
I've said and done to them.

Fly

No one will save you,
not your dead father or
your living uncle,
not the man who plants
his body inside you at night,
not the stranger
in town, at the park, or on the bus.

No net beneath you now;
some man you once knew
sliced away the woven rope;
you can only grasp at

air. Hope a wooden swing finds
your waiting hands. Jump
and hope to fly.

On the Road to Wendell, a Rainbow

Arches across the sky, of all places—
Wendell, town of rednecks and churches,
tobacco fields and gas stations. And a man
asks me if I've made a wish.

I haven't even seen a rainbow in decades,
wonder does this mean change is now sliding in
after flat archless lows—the deaths, the swooning
spectrum of departures. The selling off of colorless days.

And what would I wish for anyway?
For a kiss? To lie down in a bed, a slumbered haze
hip against hip with a man I have yet to
meet or to wed, for the reaching of goals? Well,

this evening just before dusk it was quite enough
that swell of red, green, violet light
in front of my eyes finding me
on that road to a town called Wendell.

Memory's Innkeeper

I apologize, dear guests,
nostalgia blows inside your room
and there is nothing
to do to carry it away for good;
mops have other uses.

It leaks in through the ceilings,
no one told me there were holes
in the inn's roof or inside my own head,
the past pours out this way
when no one suspects.

No matter how many nights I practice
biting this tongue, names of jilted lovers
slip away. Roll up your pants. The flood
is coming. Footmen are waiting by the beds
while the man and woman make love.

You will not drown
in reminiscence; close your eyes
and all will soon be dry again. I will patch
the roof, sweep away slippery faces from the floors,
dry out the bucket for now, dear guests.

This Is Your Life

Place your hand in the fire;
imagine it is a river
that can only burn the skin
of one who fears and sees flame.

Jump out of the plane.
No parachute. Fall
and grab what you need
on the way down.

You are a single petal
cast free from the flower;
you will land on another
stem and thrive.

You are the feather
of a bird, one feather
that can fly because
it remembers flight.

Leave the house
you built years before;
the ground descends
beneath bare feet.

There is a river
and long ago
you taught yourself
how to swim.

Spell of Larimar

Because I could not capture
the sky
inside my fist, I wanted it –
this celestial stone,
merger of heaven and clouds, unearthly
rock of blue-white streaked beauty
thrown down to mortals from the Gods.

Dominican gem, Caribbean rarity,
stone from the sea.
When I shut my land-stranded lids to midnight,
I dream of it
dancing before the stars
like old lovers.

Then I scour larimar sites, searching
for the perfect one—stone of clouds
and sky and sea, to wear, possess
beneath my pulsing breath.

Stinger

Gray worry worms eat away light
tonight and there is no way to know what
those hands pressed against the moon
really mean, always folding and unfolding
the palms of reason and dismay.

Perhaps I am witness to some test
displayed before the green fades
from the grass again. The moths
are long gone, and soon the geese
will leave too.

      Still,
the bee that stuck its stinger
in my August red blush flesh instigates
arm throbbing months later: belated pain.
Where can this body turn for answers?
No books or papers can cure or alleviate
such a thing
as this hanging half-hinged heart.

I dream away the geese, and the bees continue
to buzz around disrupting the present with the past.
The stinger will emerge tomorrow morning
on my sheets, and all those tears will rise up
toward tomorrow's moon in a water spout.

Suspended in blackness, hands opening and closing
spilling salty rivers in the night sky,
illuminated by stars that cannot blink away sorrow
or extinguish their own light.

Grief Basket

I set this grief inside a basket and push it down
the stream, then watch the dead kicking up the black
blanket. Some grown woman down the river
will pick up this basket, hold
that blanket in her arms. I had to let it go –
it kept me awake all night with those incessant
cries, with the shaking of that death rattle
last breath. I had nothing left to feed its greedy mouth.
Some other daughter will raise up this grief,
silence the screams. I'm done with it.

But why, oh why, does your deep voice still linger
here, rattle me so? Your voice swells against
the walls of my house early and late. There
in the tub and bouncing off my dreams.
I hold my palms over my ears, but that baritone
hum emerges from inside and pours out.

There is nothing new to gain from this voice,
or from this moving backwards. I've traveled here
through every patch of this childhood yard,
traversed dirt and weeds. I have climbed every
willow and oak tree, examined every fallen
knotted branch, held every found stone up
to the sun. Inclusions are everywhere. Years ago,
my mother unclipped the quilt and laundry
from the rope-woven clothesline.
She hung the family fabric wet in the yard.
I feel the pinch of the wooden pins on my skin.
She no longer unclips the shirts and pants, drops
the laundry inside the basket. That same basket floated
down the river.

I want to walk forward, out of this yard, this neighborhood,
this hometown, but I no longer know how to move
these given legs in any direction but backwards.
I am planted in this place, this town, this yard
of the bi-level home where we all once lived.
My feet have grown roots, my arms – branches.
Arms ache from reaching away from here.

I still want what I wanted. For the bird that fell
from the branch to keep breathing, for his wings
to heal, to watch him grow and end up in flight
toward the clouds. So I stand in the yard, conjure him
broken and breathless on the ground.

I am not broken I whisper to the grass. I have muttered
this phrase for years. I no longer believe the words
dropping from my own lips. I do not believe in heaven.
Dead is dead. That bird has been gone thirty years.
I keep his feathers in my back pocket. I see his feathers
clipped to the laundry line. His blood leads to the river.

Here is the basket floating away in the river. I watch
it leaving, but that deep voice inside my head will not
float away. I close my eyes and race to a hospital room.
Now the bed is empty. It is too late. Too late for holding
my father's hand. Too late for whispering my own
breath in his ear. On a white sheet – a single feather.

The bird's wing never healed. The bird never lifted up
into the sky. I dream that he did. Every night that bird
finds flight. Every night my father rains words inside my ears.

I am the basket holding our family clothes dried
in July's sun. The wooden clothespins have been
collected. I am clinging to the quilt, to my brothers' shirts
and my mother's skirts. I throw myself in the river
and float away carrying this grief that cannot sink or swim.

Dream Rant

What does it mean
that I dream of leaving you?
Last night in my dream life
I yelled out *I want a divorce.*
When I woke, I couldn't look
you in the eye.

Sometimes at night you're not
my husband, or it's you
but with a different face,
voice, or body. Like a Colorforms
dream husband where body and features
get switched. Sometimes I date
other men at night, but half-way
through dinner and wine guilt
rises in my throat and a voice
whispers, *Hey, you're married,
you're not supposed to date.*
I wake with a smile on my face,
guilt moist between my legs.

I've read that dreams don't mean
what you think they do. If a chicken squawks
during shut-eye, you have to ask:
What do chickens mean to you?
Are you afraid of chickens? Perhaps
the chicken is your angry father.
Does your dad have a nose like
a chicken's beak? Or maybe you just
dozed off while chickens clucked
during a sitcom or commercial.

Maybe I ask my dream husband
for a divorce because my biggest fear
is that I'll end up like my own mom –
divorced in her forties, alone the rest
of her life. I wish I knew.

When I began therapy years ago
I asked my therapist *Do you do dreams?*
she shook her head and I was crushed
but too afraid to tell her about my disappointment
because in my waking life I avoid expressing
myself aloud. I'd rather discuss the nightlife
than my waking, walking daily calendar.

I used to recall every single dream, but now
there are only thin slices that drop in from time to time,
then slip away like rice paper that dissolves on your tongue.
When I dream in color I wonder if that means
I'm artistic. Maybe I'll become a potter
or glassblower in my eighties. I could talk all day
about my dreams: the one where I fly, the one where
I flee from a faceless man, the one where people
I've lost touch with sit on my porch;
still children, they play jacks.

There are two recurrent dreams:
one about kicking a soccer ball but it never finds the net.
In the second one, I return to my college P.O. box
to find hundreds of letters from friends who have been
trying to contact me, by sending mail to that small box
but I've forgotten the combination.

All far more interesting than my real life. Today
for example, I drank two cups of strong coffee,
drove the kids to school, walked the dog
then watched the news.

I look forward to closing
my eyes at night, boarding the REM plane and traveling
to countries and planets filled with the unknown
and uncensored.

Maybe if I dream of leaving you I am thinking I should
and my conscious mind, though years behind, will
figure it out eventually.

They say you can't die in your dreams, but I've
fallen to my death over a hundred times.

My grandfather visited me in my sleep after
he died, sent messages to deliver to my mom.
While alive, he worried about her after the divorce.
It makes perfect sense that he'd worry
in the afterlife too. I wish he would come back
and tell me why I keep asking for a divorce
in my dreams, and tell me why that damn chicken
recently clucked his argument in my own voice
then stabbed my mouth with his sharp beak
drawing black blood that leaked
onto my bed, covering up the truth.

Train, Remains

There is only blackness and
the edges of photo, stair-step heads,
faces of three known children.

My arms grasp for stars but no light
finds these fingertips and that man
united with on a train—stranger turned

husband, he walked backwards
caboose by caboose until
we became strangers again.

The lingering wheels of the train spin away
at night and those photos have
formed cuts on my fingers.

Fingers stuck in both before and after,
time cannot be motionless, but only blood runs
forward, my own blood and their father's blood

that travels through their thriving veins
our children, myself and the stranger—
this in the end is what remains.

At the Midnight Carnival

Join me at the crimson carnival tent
said the midget beneath the star-flecked night.
I ignored him and kept leaning
against the pole wanting my hips
to join the circus, for night's elephant momentum
to stone roll forward; what I meant
to say back was that hours are lost
inside every circus tent, that the satin-clad
trapeze artists leap and spin indecision
and slim torsos across the air, but outside
the moon waits for empty stand clarity,
for stars to tunnel through darkness,
for the knife throwers to settle inside
their pointless silent beds. I reach out
my elastic palm and fingers to clasp the other
flying hand, but only air is there to meet me.

Drill, Baby

Everything becomes funny here
in the dentist's chair as nitrous
oxide flows through my nose;
even the drill doesn't make me
quiver, deliver me from monotony.
Bring it on, I say, for an entire year of days
dark sky has thrown real meteors
my way. They have burned my bed
and body in ways I never imagined.
Hope has been mined away from
my heart and tossed beyond seeing.

I hum over the grind of the drill, trying
to find a workable future in created notes.
Dirty and dry a man at the happy hour bar
orders a martini. *Dirty and wet* I mouth.
I am no longer here. I have not been present
all year anyway. No anchor. Men drift
in and out of my bed. One body drills
my body, faceless blurs of testosterone
containing shells. Who cares. *I like my men
hard,* I reply when one asks me what I want.

Drill my teeth. My body soon will remain
open. Drill the ground. I recall the baby
bird fallen from the nest. The rest is just
noise and remembering. I set that bird
inside the earth's dirt cradle, watched
dirt and rain mingle and turn to muddy lid.

Above me in the dentist's seat, eight dots circle
and twirl into stars. Every single thing has been
about these stars that become the body
of a small bird that I still grieve for.
There is no reprieve from this first loss.

Museum of Lost Wishes

Enter the museum of wishes, clutch
a star and let it burn your hand, release
it, watch it swish and twirl across
the air, then travel room to room.

At night the janitor hums and runs his broom
along the floor and gathers crumbs
of disappointment, dots of accumulated yearning.
He spills burnt ash remnants in the trash.

What will you learn here? Release
all that you once desired, spit honey
from your tongue. Your lovers
left you years before. All turns bitter,

then wooden framed. Your heart no longer pumps
with blood or want; all God-painted cells turn to stone.
In the end there is just a metal plaque
nailed on the museum wall marking

your single masterpiece now on display. The colored
places and faces you never found.
The janitor will return to sweep away
any clues or crumbs you left behind.

This After Place

Here worms do not turn
into colorful butterflies, and stars
never appear at dark.

Horses do not gallop
in yellow-flower-dotted parks
children do not skip and play.

No, not a dream but daily
waking after a certain person
leaves. There are many ways

of vanishing. Some leap
off a bridge into a bay; some drive
too fast and strike a metal pole.

Some souls simply saunter out
the door after telling you they do not
and never will love you.

Accounting (9 Dates in 9 Days)

1. His mother was a paranoid schizophrenic.
He is the 7th of 7 children and raised by his siblings.
When his mother told him information, his father took it back
by saying *Don't listen to her, she's crazy*.
He says that you remind him of his older sister.

2. Restaurant clatter tunnels in silence and you recognize
the signs of the pre-faint: your date's mouth moves
but you hear no words. About to pass out, you stare
at your water and wonder if he drugged you or if
you are reacting to too much MSG in the Kung Pao
chicken. He takes your pulse and you manage to remain
upright and conscious. You call a friend on the way home
to talk you through the drive. You didn't like him anyway.

3. He drives all the way from Jacksonville, over two hours,
smart Navy pharmacist guy who sounds smart and funny
on the phone, but at the table at Ragazzi's he reminds you
of your tactless uncle when he flosses his teeth
right there in front of you. *Really,* you exclaim.
You box up your leftovers and feed them to your dog.

4. He's short. Really short. He lied about his stature—
two inches shorter than his profile said. Did he really think
you wouldn't notice? This leads to a short date.

5. He seems okay and hugs you goodnight, praises your beauty
in the parking lot of the mall after buying you dinner. He asks
why you haven't been scooped up yet. You shrug.
You don't want to admit you've just been dumped. He begs
you to go out again, then goes silent. A week later his photo
appears again on the dating site beside a different name. WTF?

6. You can't see past his really crooked yellow teeth.
Two are missing. His parents must have been poor or negligent.
You stare at absence and don't hear a thing he says.

7. He's dull but tall and has a nice face. But by the end
of an hour, you are so bored that you want to run away.
No wonder his wife left him.

8. He talks *ad nauseam* about running a half marathon,
about the details of running trails, about every single run
he's taken in a year. He asks you why you don't run.
You try, tactfully as you can, to tell him your giant boobs
would hurt. He doesn't seem to understand. When he shows
you his tattoo he got related to running, you lose interest.
You hate tattoos on middle-aged men.
What are they trying to prove?

9. You can't see beyond his blonde toupee.
It reminds you of dolls.

Exhaustion sets in. Yes, you ate 9 free meals, but now pieces
of you are vanishing. You think you will be alone forever.

Make No Exceptions

Not for the man with young children
or the one who says he only cheated
once, no not him. Once a cheater always
a cheater. Stick to your careful list
even when a man calls you a snob
when you tell him you will not date him
because he lacks a degree—it's not about
the degree—it's about persistence and
long-term security; it's about stick-to-it-ness.
You owe nobody an explanation.
You get to choose; refuse to spend
another 22 years with a man you do not love.

Pining for Old Lovers

He desires a perpetual state
of yearning, pining
for spring in winter,
then wanting winter in summer.

How fickle
the chorus sings.

But he does not hear
lyrics or notes,
nor does he care.

Desire is strongest
when longing for ghosts.

Collage: Legs and Arms

Beneath the black crayon roof
a mother, a father, a child.
Today, a red crayon scribbles
over the clover in the yard,
the pine trees, and the mother's
face. The wife no longer holds
the husband's hand or a wedding
band.

*

Years ago, this outlined wife
held her grandpa's hand; they walked
the hospital wards, as he completed
rounds, scent of bleach and sickness
overwhelming her tiny nose and mouth.
Her eyes wandered over blanketed
laps on the amputee floor;
she searched for limbs to find absence.

*

That young hand tries to draw
the missing legs, arms, feet.
Torsos roll down the halls, and she wants
to turn away from vanished limbs.
For years, arms, legs, feet appear
at midnight behind her closed lids.

*

After the ice storm, the crashing noise,
the knocking off of house edges and borders,
gutters and soffits, that horse limb pierced
through the white ceiling. Leg without body.
Then a leaking shower pan, the ceiling opening
to damage. Her son's teenage leg jutting through
the tile, a single kick through the living
room ceiling, birth through drywall.

   *

This morning a body beside her, not her husband.
Arms and legs and torso,
a beating heart belonging to flesh
she knows but does not know.
She twists her body of breasts
and legs, twining around this male body
until they form a single question mark.

   *

She traces lines with her adult fingers,
this hand where lines were imprinted
before sliding out of her mother's body,
no way to change the climbing vines
on her palm.

About the Author

Maureen Sherbondy's poems have appeared in numerous publications, including *Calyx, Feminist Studies, European Judaism, 13th Moon, Comstock Review, Cairn, Crucible, The Roanoke Review,* and the Raleigh *News & Observer.* Her poems have won first place in The Deane Ritch Lomax Poetry Prize, *The Lyricist* Statewide Poetry Contest, The Carrie McCray Poetry Award, and The Hart Crane Memorial Poetry Award.

Maureen lives in Raleigh, NC. She has a BA degree from Rutgers University and an MFA degree from Queens University of Charlotte. She teaches English at Alamance Community College. Her books include *After the Fairy Tale, Praying at Coffee Shops, The Slow Vanishing, Weary Blues, Scar Girl, The Year of Dead Fathers, Eulogy for an Imperfect Man,* and *Beyond Fairy Tales.* Visit her website at *www.maureensherbondy.com*